AF335733

little mouse

poems by

Bill Griffin

MAIN STREET RAG PUBLISHING COMPANY
CHARLOTTE, NC

Acknowledgments:

The author wishes to thank the following editors and journals where these poems first appeared:

Cave Wall: "bread," "flight"
Iodine: "garbage," "rain"
Main Street Rag: "eighteen," "falling"
Parting Gifts: "evidence," "gods," "meadow," "rock,"
    "something," "wildness"
Pinesong (NCPS): "love"

ISBN: 978-1-59948-275-0

Produced in the United States of America

Main Street Rag
PO Box 690100
Charlotte, NC 28227
www.MainStreetRag.com

for my family, all 6,865,902,157 little mice of you

Contents

mouse [**n.** *mous;* Old English *mus,* from Latin *mûs*]
1. a creature at once ubiquitous and unobserved
2. male or female, young or old, parent or child
3. the *every-person*

little mouse
(love)

This is hard to say: I'm not sure
          of you. Every night another storm
scatters our nest; in the aftersilence
I practice words that would make us right,
but in the morning they scurry and flit

like little mice, gone. What hawk's shadow
          am I afraid of? That our struggle
will abrade the husk that once cracked allows
something green to sprout?
Or that one of us will flit and scurry, gone?

Carve away the confusion about what little
          we've made and may make, cut out every
what might have been, what might become, write
them into another poem named (hunger)
or (parent). What does that leave?

I'm not sure. When will I confess
          what I'm not sure of is me?
This nest is a straggle of shreds
and promises. This nest is now.
Come sit beside me in the moment.

**little mouse
(gods)**

They are barefoot and smile
no cat's prey welcome, no sharp
        canines; they clad the gold
of their perfection in flannel, denim;
they defer to small and gray

with no awareness
of their deference. They are so high
        that low is an abstraction;
they give and have no name
for giving. How to remain jealous

of such? How to retain
the urge to gnaw their hem?
        When I bleed they heal, but when
the trap that twists
and eats me is a ragged blade

of days and years and no escape only
endure, then they see from a cloud,
        confused. They bend to touch
this thing they thought was them,
and then they cry.

little mouse
(rain)

It falls on the just and on
the unjust. I crouch at the edge
of the picnic, mouth half full of
cold piecrust; gray regret streams
          through my whiskers. I mutter

why me? High noon, a hill
above Galilee, you rob a stone
of its threadbare shade; hell waits
at your shoulder, but heaven grumbles,
          reneges. Grace descends,

chill crystal. You raise little paws
and cry not me, not worthy;
healing and salt mingle
down your face. Not everything
          that makes us tremble is punishment.

Not every judgement condemns.
Neither then do I judge you nor withhold
what just might cleanse us both.
Why do I say regret? Isn't all this
          still a picnic?

**little mouse
(wildness)**

God, you have left nothing
out here. The empty sky full
        of stars beyond reach,
the lightning-creased snag, its curled lichen,
my small gray corpse visited

by wasps. Where does the narrow
trail lead? I climb—it's steep.
        Do I desire pain? At the summit
a few red spruce left behind to shepherd
the confusion of blueberries. Waxwings buzz

reconciliation. Mountain replies,
foggy breath. We the company
        of small things notice that rot spawns
beetles; at the wake of fallen giants,
blackberries. This prayer:

When I pass may I never disdain
what remains. Hold perfectly still
        and the red squirrel
investigates *me*. God, here
you have left nothing out.

                                    Bill Griffin

little mouse
(salt)

No thanks, I don't want a bite
of your country ham. No red-eye gravy.
I'll stick with bacon: I can pick it up,
        it's crisp, always raises my pressure
just enough. Exactly like those poems

you used to write, Raven and Bear,
each voice like mist rising in purple hemlocks,
like riffles over old, old stones,
        and my favorite *Peromyscus leukopus*,
little whitefoot who chews and keeps chewing

into the sapstream, into the heart.
Stone. Sap. Heart. I get it. But why
do you say we're all of us little
        mice? How can one voice be mother, baby,
father? Do you have to make me

a metaphor? Feed me something
I can recognize as food. But since you ask,
I will try just a spoonful
        of your grits, no sugar this time.
Earth. Food. Salt. Pass it, please.

little mouse
(bread)

The simplest things conceal the greatest
mysteries. First, this oak: three hundred years
hunkered on the mist-grazed ridge. Dew-
          jeweled whiskers grayer than mine.
Ten feet up, rooted in the broad embrace

of its branching, an orange flame blooms,
wild azalea; its own entanglement, a mouse's nest.
Next, home: you spread a damp cloth
          across the wide crock and a musk
of blessing expands to fill the kitchen,

tiny lives expanding in the dough.
And one more miracle: tomorrow the warm loaf
you carry to the altar becomes
          forgiveness. I chew mercy. I swallow.
Tiny lives; the great and ancient life;

my soul small, whiskered, gray become
acceptable. Now this prayer: invited I invite.
Come into me all you lives, expand
          my heart, become in me an oak, a warm kitchen.
The simplest things reveal the greatest.

Bill Griffin

little mouse
(parent)

Does it have five toes? is all
I want to know, this pygmy club
        that thumps me in the ribs. And whole
backbone, braincase, all painted for me
by the sonic brush—I see

you in the womb, God claims,
and does the Maker see the twisted
        path of days your little foot
will toddle? When all I know
is your shadow self, that restless

weight that tugs us forward, I can paint
pink sunrise for you, cloudless afternoon. But now
        you're here!—mousepup you thrash naked
for the teat, and in too few days you crawl,
you walk, you run so fast that soon

you pass beyond where I can see.
What is the midnight sleeplessness, the bruise
        so near my heart that makes me long
to count your toes? O God, show me my baby's
heart, that it will be whole. And more . . . be full.

**little mouse
(hello)**

Is this the hunger squeak
that drowses up from your milky world
into ours? Or the night squeak
        of cold toes pushed past
the flannel of their brothers?

Afternoon ticks away like squeaks
of cradle rocking on uneven oak,
the neighbor's westie barks
        from a distant realm. A squeak
of smile brief as sunclouds—O!

let us all sleep and wake
and sleep again to dream of little mouse
who retells the earth story
        in sharp-toothed tenor, truth that swaddles
each one of us at the breast

of one mother. Slow and constant
mosslight seeps beneath our lids, we see
with lips, with tongue, with cheek,
        our restless small squeakings
now quieted. And fed.

                                         Bill Griffin

little mouse
(something)

There's a reason for it
when my baby cries. I reason
         it out—how long
since he nursed; check wet,
check cold, check bubbles. Whatever

seems to help, but give him
something. There is no cry that has no
         reason; every one requires its big
or little something, never
nothing. So I recognize a lie

when something cold and stinging
is about to thunder from those clouds
         around your face
and you say it's nothing. Somewhere
a naked mousepup squeaks

for his lost teat, reason
enough for any one of us to return
         to nest, to listen
for the silent cry, to offer never
nothing, always something.

little mouse
(struggle)

I wish you wouldn't lay me here
          on my belly. I refuse
to settle into the coverlet, to fill
my nose with lint, to rest.
This grunt, this squirm, this wriggle

and wail are not to please you but only
          because I want to *see*. What
has become of it, this universe
I was the center of? My first gasp
was followed by a cry; between milk

and sleep and colors must there be pain?
          When I see muscles tense, little mice
of your desire, I am part of all the
urgency. I can't give up. What?
Who is saying that? I barely know *da-da*,

it will be twenty years before
          I say *conflate*. The story
is still being written. Simply say of me
I often struggle, and many times
I lift my head.

                                              Bill Griffin

little mouse
(hunger)

O the soft white yeasty sin
of it! When I was just a pup I stole
a piece of bread from your kitchen,
hid it behind the sofa to be sure
         I'd always have it, just in case.

The next day it was hard—
O bitter loss! The fear
of someday almost starving.
And so then the Christmas candy stashed
         behind the socks 'til Easter, and that

'til Halloween, then that forever—
what you eat you can't keep. Now
the August figs ripen so fast I can't
consume them all (without getting sick);
         I slice their pink seduction, lay

them on a tray to dry. Sunheat
drinks their moisture, leaves the sweet.
Something to hold, something not to lose.
On the longest night I take one out
         and chew it, so slowly, so slow.

little mouse
(breath)

I am reading a poem while you undress
         for bed, and inside the poem
the breath of the world catches,
holds perfectly still at the possibility
that the reader might discover

one beautiful thing, then releases
         with a sigh like roses
because it is becoming
true. Outside the poem
the breath of the world explores

the corners of the house with a touch
         like wind. I look up.
You already have your pajamas on
(I have missed your nakedness),
the pale flannel with clusters of pink

roses like someone's grandmother
         would wear. Then I remember. You are
someone's grandmother, our own
little mouse, whose breath is roses
and the world becoming true.

                                    Bill Griffin

little mouse
(falling)

You would have grabbed him, caught
his broken harness before the misstep
          on the railroad trestle. Pulled
him back from his hell, your grief.
And you're still pulling, or trying anyhow

to pull some kind of joy into this hour.
No, not joy, just any something
          out of the well of nothing
where you've fallen. What makes us all
so heavy? Why can't I be a mouse who leaps

past loss, the air of unencumbrance
a cushion beneath my care-less
          glide? You and I know otherwise.
It isn't gravity that binds
two souls together. Your pull is more

than fear of losing. I want us
to fall together—what we're all made for
          (if I'm honest with my Maker)
is to embrace, to care, to fall
and never ask how far.

little mouse
(bullet)

Are any of us innocent?
His son's bullet was shaped
like an old Buick that lunged
into the intersection, no seatbelts,
        ten seconds from home. Almost hello

turned goodbye. My father's was a single slow
cell that twisted, then faster; cut it away
but it claws back; burn it,
poison it—a cat's black shadow
        still crouches in our night.

Your bullet, boy, has become
the thing itself, mouseweight of lead,
toxic metal, one exclamation and then
silence. Innocence. Are any of us
        not? And your mother's

is the door she opens
to discover you there, that cold
and final door she must
open and keep opening until
        the end of bullets.

                                        Bill Griffin

little mouse
(friends)

How long does it take *forget*
          to limp along after
forgive? Are you the same
creature to whom I wished
such grievous harm? Black claws

of guilt to rake your soul,
          misfortune's wicked plow
to cleave your nest?
Evil one, how have you grown so
bafflingly companionable?

Or have I limped along so far to find
          snowdamp softens even thistle's
prick? Foolishness! I vowed
forever barbs and dissonance.
More than years, it requires

shared verses to perfect the rhyme.
          Now it's time for you to play
your blue harmonica while I sing.
When ever did we hurt each other? When
did we hate? I forget.

little mouse
(wind)

A hundred of us have climbed
        this old trail. Toppled giants sprout
epiphytes, moss eats bark,
one wide stump's signature
in chainsaw script: 9/22/89. Hugo.

A thousand of us blown
        from our nests, dervish Girls
and Boys from East Atlantic
draw back gale fists and smack us
silly. Ten thousand wander

answerless, even forget the question.
        A sip of water? White bread,
two tablespoons of peanut butter?
Someone to tell me everything
is going to be all right?

My babies, blind, naked, are they safe?
        Can I recover what the living storm
devours? Will I recognize my home?
And now a million? All of us
have leaned into that wind.

                                                                Bill Griffin

**little mouse
(garbage)**

What we throw away:
shall I make a list?
The brown spot and the whole
apple around it;
       the purple spot

and the addict's arm
and the whole man. Mostly
what's hard to look at or easy
to look past. An empty wallet full
       of bus rides home; the child

crying in the detergent aisle;
a dark man who laughs
in another language. Thinking
we can have what we've killed
       to keep. And my soul, too,

is small and gray
as all the rest. Yesterday
I nibbled crumbs and was happy
until someone told me
       they were crumbs.

little mouse
(blame)

If only you
        hadn't distracted me I
wouldn't have run into him.
If only you would quit
getting mad every time

I make a mistake I
        wouldn't keep making it.
If only you never
reminded me I'm not perfect I
might agree with you.

If only you could tell
        I always bristle to make myself
big when I'm especially
small and gray. If only
you'd concede it's my nature

to chew things, spit out,
        leave holes. If only I
could admit I might be
to blame, then maybe you
would forgive me.

                                        Bill Griffin

little mouse
(cookie)

Handful of gray flakes, dry
as the forsaken stalks that bore them,
        begging for salt, sugar, left
with all the personality of dust—
oatmeal. And who else besides

an advert copy writer really thinks
of sunshine when she eats
        a raisin? Eggs, butter—staples,
no spotlight, unglamourous
as back row tenor

in the chorus. But mix
and perfect them with physics,
        chemistry—even a mouse's fragment
becomes evidence enough
for intelligent design.

And you, my sometimes half-baked
confection, the parts of your sum
        may barely wring yawns
from the gods, but your altogether
is my sweet favorite.

little mouse
(meadow)

Bluestem, red top, deer-tongue,
foxtail, the grasses extract
          usury from sunlight
and invest it in seed. A place
of contempt, to say they've gone to?

What is so disgusting about
untended? Business as usual
          for the white crab spider tense
in her thistle, angling
for skippers. I'll risk poison

for a meal of nectar. Do I really
have a choice? Should I go
          to law school? My little body
struggles to creep through the fescue
of sameness. Other paths

are what I myself must press between
the clumps of tallgrass, unpredictable but
          paths nonetheless. Red top.
Bluestem. My soulcolor fed by seed
that sifts down from heaven.

                                              Bill Griffin

**little mouse
(smoke)**

What's scary is I don't know how much
I don't know: you advise me never light my fire
with paper—the sparks may rise
          into disaster. Stick my hand
above the damper—what secrets cling there

up the flue? Later, a patter in the rafters
like ticking claws on toes on hordes
of mousepaws—don't tell me that's
          the first lick that flickers in the creosote,
soon to drink and spew and shake

the house like wolves. I'll pretend
there's nothing there. The lies that matter
are the ones you tell yourself. I'm good
          at looking past the unvoiced fire
that consumes you from inside. I can convince

myself between us everything is cool.
At least I could. Lately I suspect just how little
I know. Might knowing the not knowing
          let me find the spark that could quicken us?
Is it too late to save us from the ashes?

little mouse
(rock)

Can't call it stone, something too elegant
in that word, chip away letter
by letter to discover David or
Cupid & Psyche; could never polish
          this one up and invite

the critics to admire. Nope, just a chunk,
slab, handcrag, some unnameable
mineral the mother lode tossed aside.
If it was flatter I'd skip it twelve hops
          down Elkin Creek, set

a record. If sharper I'd strike sparks
against steel, set a fire. Bigger, I'd stash seeds
under, set for winter. You kidding? I'll just keep
this lump as is, remind me of a place
          I've been, maybe someday

go back there, take you with me, both of us
all chipped away, past splash
and sparks. Can't call you stone
or scion (too elegant), not offspring or heir,
          not progeny. Just son.

                                        Bill Griffin

little mouse
(flight)

If A then B. Midnight, the heron is taut
as a tendon; the lance of his beak prophesies
a bullseye in the shallows. Downtown heron —
choose to hunt by streetlight this creek
          that wanders past rec center,

library, under the road where I walk home
late from work. I wouldn't have chosen
to walk; I totalled my options. At last
it's down to this. Make one choice
          and it strips you of all the rest

(and not to choose counts
as your choice). Heron spots me, tenses
for the leap that will launch him
into the open mouth of night.
          And then he doesn't. If not A then not B.

Back home you nurse our little mouse, hope
he'll sleep away the darkness, hope you'll see me
in one piece. I'm waiting on this heron.
Is there any hope to spare? This time
          maybe just enough to fly?

little mouse
(morning)

Darkness is when cries
go unanswered. Are all
the ones I love asleep? Blue
          lightning, police cruisers
thunder to the wreck

I've made of everything
you've given me. Don't I deserve
to lose? No kestrel diving
          out of the sun, no pounce,
no rend—in darkness I confess

I chose the steps
that carried me into night.
No gods, no fate, no
          inborn compulsion, no travesty
of justice, I juggle those answers

all day long but now
here I am with no one. What?
Someone who loves me
          is calling? Could it be I see
a little light?

                                        Bill Griffin

little mouse
(evidence)

Listen, it's there again,
      bone tremor like a footfall
on deep moss after midnight,
not my ears that hear, my heart
feels it. Not my eyes,

they're closed, but light enters
      like sun filtered through miles of leaves
to find earth's one white
petal. You want to see
a footprint, count the round toes, claws

flexed or full extension. You would sniff
      the imprint, scribble genus . . . species,
publish your theories and turn up
your nose at mine. Can you write me
an equation for hope? A hand

hovers above my shoulder lightly (un-)
      touching. In the domain of mice
all large things are death. Why
am I convinced my life depends
on the one thing I can't prove?

little mouse
(stuff)

I own a book I've never read. OK
        OK, a couple dozen. More. (And not all
of them poetry, either.) Will I ever really
excavate the pile beside my bed? and meanwhile
half dot com keeps calling to me.

On the shelf a CD gathers dust
        unopened (*Die Fledermaus*): I meant
to sneak it into your stocking, but you
have yet to listen to the birthday's,
mother's day's, *etc.* Our rooms are full

of cetera, those other things—did I think
        I could redeem my self by filling shelves?
What is the other that this stuff replaces?
Could I survive a week without buying
anything but bread and milk?

I'm afraid to ask it: What would Jesus
        buy? In his hands he cups
a little mouse, squats beside a soup can over
a fire of twigs to brew wild beebalm tea,
another way of turning water into wine.

little mouse
(diagnosis)

Might as well be a verdict—
this letter requires my presence
in doctor's court, clinical cut-open envelope,
wound of a lab result that "we" must
        investigate. Doesn't denial insinuate

I know the truth I'm running from?
My tail is pinned to earth,
little claws scrabble but I'm
not moving. Did someone squeak?
        Am I even in this world?

My voice (or is it mine?) calls to awaken me,
tells me calmly I can do this, phones
to schedule the biopsy. More weeks
creep past but no more of that
        paralysis. Later—a good piece of me is gone

but all the bad bits too. Not hope speaking here—
I am sure. Walking scarred how come I
feel so whole? That first afternoon
I had misheard. It was your voice saying
        we can do this. We together.

**little mouse
(eighteen)**

Who is that old man lying in my bed?
          I know it must be me but I know
it isn't. Eighteen feet away the mirror
panders to myopia (glasses lying
on the bedside stand)—can that grey ghost

really be the youngster looking out
          from behind these eyes? Flip
the light out. Sleep on it. Eighteen
inches—morning shave focused close,
no problem overlooking crow's feet

and white whiskers, keep the bright
          pupils tight, crop close and leave
the big picture for tomorrow (lots
of tomorrows)—in eighteen years
I'll be seventy-five, one wise mouse,

but when I arrive there only ninety
          will be *really* old. No sweat, stay eighteen
as long as brain cams click, knee joints don't
click too loud, eyes can click
the shutter closed on that damned mirror.

                                          Bill Griffin

**little mouse
(youth)**

You're supposed to laugh with me
when I say I taught your mother English
in a one-room schoolhouse
by kerosene lantern. Ha ha, nobody
          is that old. Nobody.

And when I announce to the world
how sexy that tall poet is and maybe
a comment about his Jack Daniels voice,
maybe a mention (not too loud)
          of the tight black jeans. And always

in third person. I know the difference
between flirt and come-on. Always my bright
colors. A loose blouse over a tight bodice. Stories
about the old days, say wild days,
          how I loved it when that rat Bukowski

propositioned me and I whirled
my braless mousebody beyond his reach.
Look now, here's a photo of my granddaughter.
Just a baby, for God's sake.
          I'm not afraid. Laugh with me.

**little mouse
(goodbye)**

How frayed the cords that twitch
like fearful prey
          beneath my paper skin;
musculus runs up and back
now nearly spent, and yet

how small a knot it takes
to bind these joints
          together: I defy
gravity and grave to raise
this final weight from chair,

walk eight steps (slowly)
to the bed, turn with only
          softest moan, settle
into a nest for little mice.
May I sleep beyond the claws

of cancer's feral cat; may needles pause
from night's unceasing gnaw;
          may the heart mouse dream
a dance, a leap
before the crouching dark.

[*musculus*: Latin: diminutive of *mûs*, mouse]

                                          Bill Griffin

little mouse
(joy)

If I could write my own story it would walk
the fine damp path along Roaring River
then cross your pasture, the deepworn tread,
        observant beasts, enter the broken
gate of your back garden and out again

to the mown lawn, cross the road, keep on
walking, walking, while you
from your police car, you behind
        the counter at the diner, you who've watched
me for forty years you all call out

Hey there, Walker, Hey Little Mouse.
I won't be writing this for I have no letters
nor even telling it with my few terse squeaks
        that mostly have to do with yes. You'll have to see
my story as I pass and understand

past and future aren't even words to me,
it isn't the miles I cover between breakfast
and supper calling me back home, it isn't
        the where I've been or the where I get to,
the joy is right now and I am walking.

little mouse

(trace)

I want to leave the earth and climb
the snowbank cumulus, kick
        my boots into the billow, lean
against my sassafras stick and rise.
Rain licks the slickrock clean

of my prints, greenbriar weaves
wild drapery up the wall, hickory sprouts
        through the sidewalk. I want to leave
no trace of my passing, no more trail
than the cursive of a slender tail

in dew. Morning sun drinks that cup
and learns a word I never spoke,
        someone's new word for love. I
want to be no more I but we—creature
loam bud feather; let roots translate

the phosphorus of my dust to fruit.
If you look for me a wren calls.
        If you listen the poplar turns to honey
in the sky. Drink deep this cup. I want
to leave the earth to you.

                                                        Bill Griffin